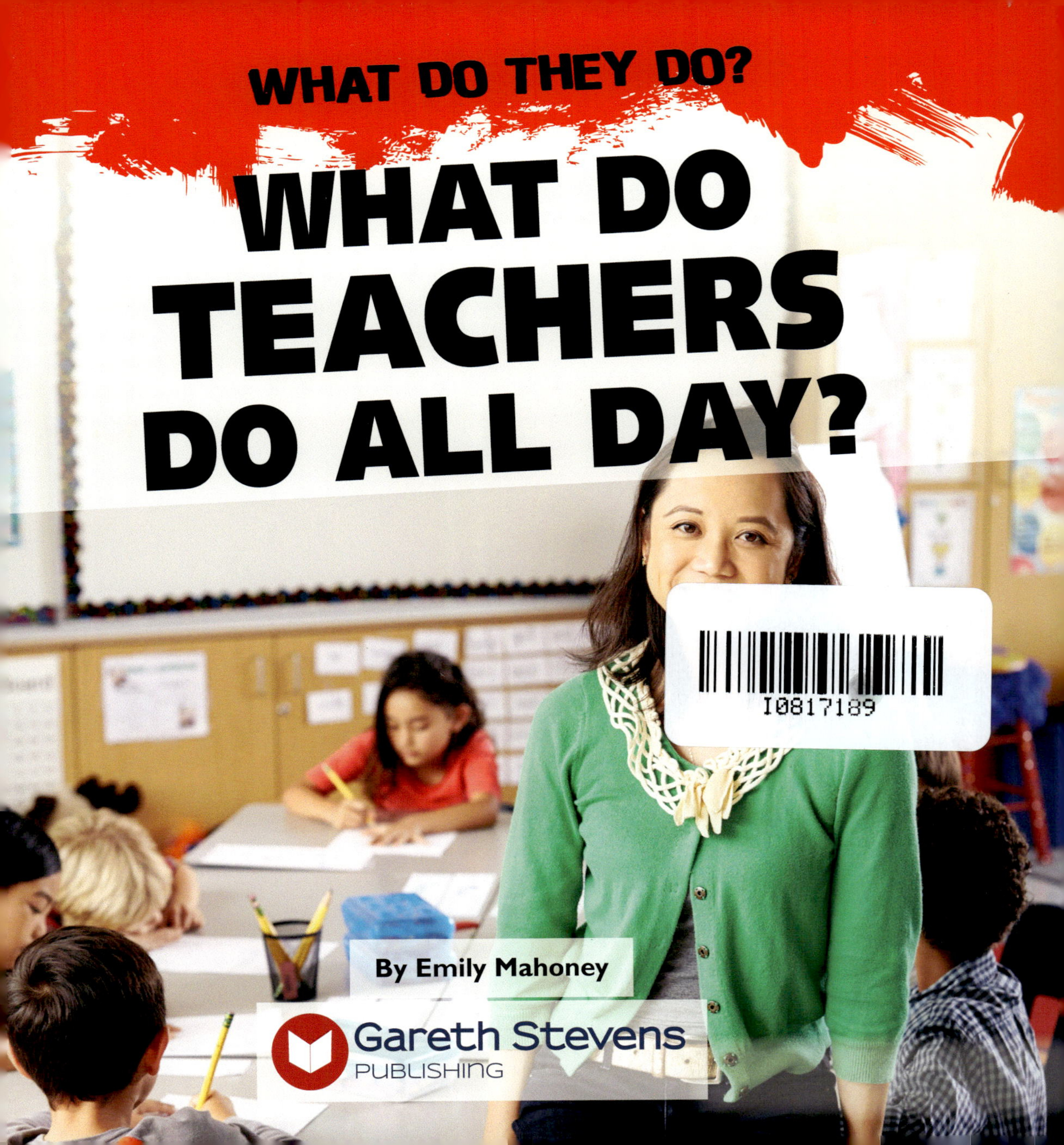

WHAT DO THEY DO?

WHAT DO TEACHERS DO ALL DAY?

By Emily Mahoney

Gareth Stevens
PUBLISHING

Please visit our website, www.garethstevens.com. For a free color catalog of all our high-quality books, call toll free 1-800-542-2595 or fax 1-877-542-2596.

Library of Congress Cataloging-in-Publication Data

Names: Mahoney, Emily Jankowski, author.
Title: What do teachers do all day? / Emily Mahoney.
Description: New York, NY : Gareth Stevens Publishing, 2021. | Series: What do they do? | Includes index. | Contents: A busy job – Planning lessons – During the day – Different days – Conferences – Worth the effort – Glossary.
Identifiers: LCCN 2019060243 | ISBN 9781538256770 (library binding) | ISBN 9781538256756 (paperback) | ISBN 9781538256763 | ISBN 9781538256787 (ebook)
Subjects: LCSH: Teachers–Juvenile literature. | Teaching–Juvenile literature.
Classification: LCC LB1775 .M4226 2021 | DDC 371.102–dc23
LC record available at https://lccn.loc.gov/2019060243

Published in 2021 by
Gareth Stevens Publishing
111 East 14th Street, Suite 349
New York, NY 10003

Editor: Emily Mahoney
Designer: Laura Bowen

Photo credits: Series art Dima Polies/Shutterstock.com; cover, p. 1 Monkey Business Images/Shutterstock.com; pp. 5, 17 Monkey Business Images/iStock/Getty Images Plus/Getty Images; p. 7 Westend61/Getty Images; p. 9 Jianbi Chen/iStock/Getty Images Plus/Getty Images; p. 11 Inti St Clair/DigitalVision/Getty Images; p. 13 FatCamera/E+/Getty Images; p. 15 Hill Street Studios/DigitalVision/Getty Images; p. 19 Alistair Berg/DigitalVision/Getty Images; p. 21 Digital Vision/Getty Images Plus/Getty Images.

Printed in the United States of America

CPSIA compliance information: Batch #CS20GS: For further information contact Gareth Stevens, New York, New York, at 1-800-542-2595.

CONTENTS

Boldface words appear in the glossary.

A Busy Job

Being a teacher is a busy job, but it can be very **rewarding**. You might think you know what a teacher does during the day because you watch your teacher when you go to school. However, there's a lot that teachers do after school or while you aren't watching that's important too!

Planning Lessons

One of a teacher's most important jobs is to plan lessons and activities for their students. This happens before the students even come into the classroom in the morning! The teacher knows what to teach because they have learned their curriculum, or what students in that grade need to learn that year.

When a teacher plans a lesson, they have a lot to think about! They must **consider** what information their students need to learn and how to teach that information. They also need to think about how long their lesson will take, what supplies they will need, and if their students will enjoy it!

During the Day

The best part of a teacher's job is when they actually get to teach and work with their students. This might include a teacher talking about a new **topic**. They may also help students who are working together in groups. Sometimes, they **monitor** students who are taking a quiz or test.

When a teacher is working with their students, they're also **assessing** how their students are doing. They want to see if their students understand what's being taught. They're also making sure that there are no **behavior** problems and that everyone is working hard in class.

When a teacher isn't working with their students during the day, they might be doing a few different things. Sometimes, they might meet with another teacher or team of teachers to plan lessons. Other times, they may be working on grading student work or even setting up activities for the next day.

Different Days

A teacher's **routine** is sometimes changed when there are fun or different activities happening in the school. For example, an assembly may be held, or a teacher may need to attend a meeting with a parent. On really fun days, the teacher may take their class on a field trip!

Conferences

Teachers sometimes go to **conferences** to learn about different ideas and activities to try in their classroom. When this happens, they usually have to leave plans for their substitute teacher. A substitute teacher teaches the class on the day the teacher isn't there.

Worth the Effort

If you're thinking that teaching sounds like a lot of work, you're right! Teaching might be a hard job with a lot going on at any moment, but it's also exciting. The feeling of helping young students learn is worth the hard work and energy that teachers put into their job.

Anthony
Jake
Sabrina
Roy

GLOSSARY

assessing: making a judgement about something

behavior: the way a person acts

conference: a meeting where people gather to talk, learn, and make decisions

consider: to think about something carefully to make a decision

monitor: to watch closely

rewarding: producing a good feeling that you have done something important or helpful

routine: the regular way of doing something

topic: something that people learn about

FOR MORE INFORMATION

BOOKS

Polacco, Patricia. *The Art of Miss Chew*. New York, NY: GP Putnam's Sons, 2012.

Steinke, Aron Nels. *Mr. Wolf's Class.* New York, NY: Scholastic, 2018.

WEBSITES

Bookworm for Kids
www.bookworm4kids.com/
This website provides great lists of books for all ages. Teachers love when their students are great readers!

Time for Kids
www.timeforkids.com/
Time for Kids provides interesting articles for curious readers, and many teachers use it in their classrooms.

Publisher's note to educators and parents: Our editors have carefully reviewed these websites to ensure that they are suitable for students. Many websites change frequently, however, and we cannot guarantee that a site's future contents will continue to meet our high standards of quality and educational value. Be advised that students should be closely supervised whenever they access the internet.

INDEX